ella zelensky

iridescence

Ella Zelensky

indescence

ella zelensky

iridescence

Ella Zelensky

© Ella Zelensky, 2025. All Rights Reserved

i listened to
the melody and
a montage of my
life in reverse
danced before
my eyes

when i reach
one arm out
i pull it back
with the other

indescence

people open the door
but sometimes
it's under our feet
when it's too good
to be true we
overlook any deceit

ella zelensky

paraphrasing what a knife is
doesn't change what the
cut feels like

you not being there for me
is exactly how it is described
you are not there

i had to save myself from a mind
that wasn't mine

the human mind
is tormenting
though it belongs
to you
it still has a
mind of its own

ella zelensky

have we lost our minds
or have our minds lost us

it took me a while
but i finally called
out your name
you left years ago

the truth is confident
the truth doesn't hide
that is why it is unlike a lie

when you left
your shoes stayed
neatly organised
by the front door
i guess i shouldn't
keep waiting for you
to enter the house anymore
no one is coming
to fill your shoes
how could anyone else
dare to imitate you
i contemplated
throwing them away
or throwing them
at the walls
but no amount of rage
will return you to these floors
so i keep your shoes
as you left them
neatly organised by
the front door
one person and one door
that won't open for
two anymore

when i asked are you listening
and you said yes i heard you
i knew you did not care for
the difference between the two

the thing about promises is that we
depend on its fulfilment so much that
we don't notice its indefinite abstention

i liked when you
finally apologised
because i realised
i didn't want it and
that felt phenomenal

indescence

they were like seaweed
beckoning you to
come and reach for them
until they roped you in
bound your torso
arms and legs
and dragged you to
the bottom of the sea
like a spider binds
its prey and eats it alive

if i keep breaking
myself into pieces
they might turn
into soldiers
turn against me
and i'll have to
fight more of myself

indescence

the shadows
demand your presence
because they don't want
you to be seen

milestone after milestone
win after win
and still i worry that
something will go wrong
i conquer multiple stages
in my life until i'm crossing
one with a graduation cap
on my head
and still i worry that
something will go wrong
i even prove that theory wrong
by reminding myself of
everything i have done right
and suddenly
i worry that something
will go right
that something will bloom
into a whole new stage
and a whole new room
that expectations will
berate me and i'll freeze in the
face of everything i dreamed for
i will become afraid of
my own success
put an asterisk next to it
to caution people that perhaps
i am the imposter after all
milestone after milestone
win after win
and that i'll run away
from those who say yes
before that yes can even begin

we live in such an
overstimulating world
that we have even
forgotten how to
nurture our bodies
in the most instinctual
of ways

i thought that if
i thought enough
thinking would
produce progress
reflection provides
protection from
rash decisions
but eventually it
stops you from making
any decisions at all

indescence

at what point
is waiting more
detrimental
than wise

we chain our necks to grief like
it's our personality until we become
too afraid to live any differently

indescence

set the fire
her pain said
i will she replied
and so began
the burning of
the whole world
her eyes widened
into circles large
enough to fit
planet earth in
as she commanded
the sky to catch fire
and blue dipped into red

the devil wants you
to play with fire
to risk your safety
and become ensnared
by desire

indescence

do not reach the point
where you
look in the mirror
and see your
worst enemy

i was like a puddle on
the ground to them
they pointed at me
ran up with their friends
and jumped in it to
get a reaction

people are more inclined
to trash the home
the apartment
the safe place
the precious space
of a person they never
truly considered a friend

i trusted putting my life
in your hands as your
hands held the wheel
it was then that i found
out you didn't have
your license yet

sometimes people fall
so deeply into the wrong
person that they become
a missing person
unfortunately this happens
so frequently that most
never make the news

when someone calls
the chain around
their neck jewellery
there is reason
to suspect they are
being treated cruelly

petals fall off the trees at school
that witness the bullies and the bullied
every petal knows what you did
and they whisper about you in the wind

ella zelensky

no one should
laugh at you on
a very special day

indescence

a nostalgia pervades
every atom in my being
i am overcome by
feelings i see in colour
it riddles me with dread
and it's taking over my head

space and time
you say you need
space and time
and i think i need it too
i need space and time from you
the one who hurts me
who makes me feel blue
to extract myself
from the pain and
look at the real meaning
of space and time
at night i sit outside
and stare at the sky
contemplating my place
in my situation and life
this is what i needed
space and time
beyond the world of you and i
two galaxies collide
and i still feel empty inside
i am your sacrifice
you live and i die
yet i continue to run back
to you every time
you say you need
space and time
and that's the difference
between you and i
you love without love
and use the excuse of
space and time as your plight
but i am worlds away
well beyond your pace
crying tears of freedom as
i escape you at the speed of light

sometimes it is harder
to find the one
lost in their mind than
the one lost in space

ella zelensky

**a reluctant *i'm fine*
should be a telltale sign**

there once was a girl
who was a time traveller

she travelled back
to the past so many times
her grief caused
her time machine to
collapse in on itself

all alone
she cried over her eternal
stay in the past because
she failed to embrace the present

and like her long lost time machine
she collapsed in on herself too
until she turned into a skeleton
in a bed of weeds

ella zelensky

goodbye
see you soon
they said
you wave as you
pull your suitcase
through the door
and into the open
ocean in front of you

when i was young a mother we knew
walked with us along a farm
as little children
the stars smiled upon us that night
and one in particular flew by
i just saw a shooting star she said
she was the only one who did
despite all the children's efforts
to say that they did too
over a decade later she died
from cancer and sometimes
i can't help but wonder how special she
must have been for the stars to choose her
to illuminate our sky
so every time i see a shooting star
i am brought back to that farm
the night she walked in contemplative silence

ella zelensky

sometimes when
you lose someone
the closest you can
get to them is by
making a guess

sometimes
the stars make me feel lonely
they have a sadness to them
an emptiness
a disconnect
a barrier you could say
they are bright and stunning
but suddenly you feel dread
they're not as close
as they look
and they don't speak back
they only stare as your
life crumbles
sometimes when i see the stars
i am reminded of the days
i used to say something
and they simply watched
so yes
the stars are beautiful
i look up to them just like you
but sometimes i can't help
but feel more alone

i can't hear you
the noise in
my head drowns
you out

iridescence

it is uninhabitable
to live inside
an angry
little world you
crush inside
your clenched fist
let it go
let it go
let it go

ella zelensky

we fight our tears
but don't fight
for ourselves

i am scared to think of
what's underneath
these floorboards
that maybe there is
a void on the
other side that
the echo of my
footsteps has
been projecting into
have i been
walking the line
between my dimension
and another dimension
this whole time
have i been dancing
on a string
skimming past
the dark that could
swallow me whole

will i end up alone
in a big space again
an individual in a crowd
who feels like there
is no one around

iridescence

every room i walked
into was a new trap
there was no escaping
a duplicating maze

ella zelensky

i float in space
like a baby in her
mother's womb
the window beside
me looking out
onto the earth
spins like i do
gradual
vivid
enamouring
safe
simply beautiful

indescence

many centuries have seen
many people create
time capsules for the universe
we have played pianos at
global music festivals
held vigils
and celebrations
and still we do not learn
no wonder god is angry with us
the stars watch earth sadly
tired of our violence
we are marked by carnage
and corrupt leaders
we are delighted by death
but indifferent to life
we seek home in the stars
but we are so unworthy
who are we to leave the earth
and the piles of dead who
surpass the highest mountains
why have our eyes been
replaced by a mist of grey

ella zelensky

look what we have done
to resort to spaceships
wrecking and murdering
and leaving the rest
to suffer as they watch
us depart for the skies
you can turn away from it
but you can't escape it
for you will continue to see
its reflection in someone's eyes

iridescence

my heart yearns for places
untouched by human infrastructure

today i feel hopeless
one little thing goes
wrong and immediately
i discredit all my wins

indescence

i am stuck in a pit
screaming for escape
and slowly
going crazy from
my own echoes

ella zelensky

stop yelling at me
i tell my mind
enough is enough
who are you
to tell me to stop
it says back
when you are the
one who made me
like this
isn't this what
you always wanted
i am the way i am
because you programmed
me to become this way
so don't come blaming me
when you were the mastermind

how does it feel to hate yourself
they asked
murder i said
murder i shouted
the real world is different
murder someone and you get arrested
but in your inner world try to murder
yourself and you get away with it
people protect you in the real world
but in your inner world you
feed yourself to the wolves
the legal system can't stop what it can't
see
so i'm left alone with my worst enemy
and it is me

before you fall
i will catch you
one last time
stand you aside
gently
quietly
and fall off the edge
in place of you
it's the least i can do
for someone as beautiful
as you

indescence

i'm in a room
full of people
and i'm the
only one here

ella zelensky

you'll be okay
i heard someone say
almost as if they were
trying to send a message
from a different dimension
i know now that it was me
and she was right
i am okay

you would think that the
further on you live
the more you drift away
from your younger self
but i have found that
the more i have healed
the closer i get to her

ella zelensky

today i found a vase
and made a flower
arrangement out of
the pain of my past

indescence

for these moments
for each other
and with each other
we must live
so that we know
that we have lived
and can live with
how we did

what we are is afraid
we are preoccupied
by death
by suffocating
by loneliness
by darkness
we do not live with
life as the rest of the world does
one might say we are
too afraid to be alive
the truth is life and
death are old friends
who do not fear each other
let us be the bridge between
them so that we may
all hold hands together
celebrate life
and conquer what freezes us
so that we may move again
walk again
run again towards the light

indescence

i ran to the ocean
when no one
was around
screaming
but you couldn't
hear it if you saw me
i threw my arms
in the air
kicked the water
fell to my knees
wept into my hands
and then lifted
my head to the sky
eyes closed until
i felt rain on my eyelids
and when i opened
my eyes
you cast a rainbow
across the whole sky

ella zelensky

and finally my dreams happened
when i wasn't asleep

will you accept
the challenges that
come with life
are you willing
to turn from soul
to human and
to soul once more
yes
your soul said
yes
said mine
yes
said everyone
else's
i accept this life

she planted the seed
knew the tree it would
grow would outlive her
this is for my legacy
she said as she stepped back
i plant my soul into this
land as my friends
plant their own seeds
let these trees bear witness
to our people and take
care of our memory

iridescence

if i only had
three days to live
i would surely choose
to fly like the butterfly

your room is a
reflection of you
you decorate it
like you're decorating
the walls of
your mind
when you walk
into it you're walking
into your thoughts
your hopes
your dreams
and even your fears
it is one of the biggest
keys to someone
understanding a part
of you that not all
are privy to

indescence

when i'm in the car
and i see people
at the bus stop
or the train station
the world turns dark
they stand out
like galaxies
and it's as if we are
looking at one another
from a distance
but i pass by them
never able to wind
back the hands
of the clock to
see them again

ella zelensky

a stranger who comes
to love another stranger
will become a stranger
to the one who has not
yet come to love

do you ever suddenly
notice your heartbeat
and you feel shocked
that is your heart
trying to tell you
i'm here
never forget me

if you're going
to have an attitude
let it be gratitude

iridescence

there's a key that
protects a secret
they said
find it and the
world will change
so i spent my whole
life searching for
a key that didn't exist
this whole time
the key was not
in the outside world
but inside me all along

when i was fourteen
i couldn't comprehend
being seventeen or tossing
my hat in the air for
graduation day because
my priority wasn't
carrying a big beautiful
bouquet down the
school driveway
when i was fourteen
i thought life would
stay this way
but it didn't
i held a bouquet when
i graduated my bachelors
tossed my cap
began a masters degree
and have found the happiness
i was close to giving up on

indescence

why do you go
to that place
he asked
cause when
i watch the sun
rise and set
every single day
i remember that
the world is
spinning
i must know that
i am alive

ella zelensky

you will find your way
out of the snow
you won't hear the
crunch of ice under
your feet when you
make it out
because the grass
awaits you

when you complete
a puzzle
you stand back
to observe how
all the pieces create
one harmonious
picture
likewise you
should trust that
each piece life
hands to you is
meant to fit into
the overall picture
it's just a matter of
figuring out where
it serves its purpose
and knowing that
it is meant to be the
bridge to other pieces

if you stare up
at the leaves
of a tree
and move your
head slightly
you will see
a kaleidoscope
shift before your eyes

indescence

and after years
of sorrow
a laugh finally
echoed out of my soul

ella zelensky

don't stop before
you start
that is the beauty
of art
it imitates life
and you are a person
who knows what
living feels like

if you tell me it will be okay
when you are alive
that fact won't change
when you're gone
death doesn't negate
a promise
and i know you too well
to know it will be okay
if you say it will be

the clock that
ticks forward
is the clock we
feel we lose
time from
but the real clock
that ticks forward
is the one we
realise gives us
more time

when you close
your eyes
what do you see
embrace the
dark expanse
and set your
imagination free
now open them again
tell me what
do you see
do you now see the
world any differently

-ode to the dead poets society

ella zelensky

you kick yourself off the roof
stumbling in the air
before you soar to your dreams
before you know it
you are among the clouds
headed towards
the star of your destiny
to others you are simply sleeping
but you know you are wide awake

not yet fate says
a few more experiences
and then you'll be
ready for the most
beautiful realisation
of your life

if i am writing books
to go on the shelf
then am i really
writing for myself

i could say each book
is better than the last
but there is nothing
less beautiful about
my lessons of the past

when you wrote
on the blackboard
the universe came
travelling towards
my eyes
and as you spoke
i heard my potential
in your passion
it wasn't what you
saw in me
it was what i
saw in me
our classroom was
a chamber of mirrors
constantly expanding
our minds
constantly confronting
our identities
how do we grow when
we think we know
all there is to know
when you finished
writing on the blackboard
turned to the class
and said see you next time
only half of us returned

you're not behind
your friends
you're ahead of
the game
their dependence
and your independence
are not the same

i'm not beautiful
to you because
your definition
of beauty is
based on insecurity

you are intelligent
it's just the wrong people
telling you you're not

ella zelensky

when human beings judge you
for all the wrong reasons
animals judge you for all
the right ones

indescence

why is your sword
made of glass
they asked
because when
you shatter it
to pieces
you will be surrounded
by mirrors that
force you to reflect
on who you have become

she left before
the final encore
because the
audience was fake
and she didn't
want to entertain
stupidity anymore

as everyone clapped
i laughed at how ridiculous
this response was
but when everyone laughed
i found no reason to clap
we've officially lost it

-the (end of) times we live in

your sword
wasn't meant to
swear allegiance
to you
it was always waiting
for someone like me

indescence

she was a friend of the forest
it takes a kind heart to be

it is brave to be
the counter argument
the whistleblower
the pioneer
it is brave to say
i am here

indescence

i have faced rejection
upon further inspection
people can't tolerate introspection
or when they look at your face
and see their own reflection
the true are thrown to the floor
or locked behind a door and are
made to feel they don't
fit in anymore
i have faced a crowd of judgement
looked it straight in the eyes
but no one cares when
the different one cries
so i took loneliness by the hand
and walked forward instead
ruffled my dress and placed
my fallen crown back on my head

you saw it as the
voice of treason
but i saw it as the
voice of reason

indescence

it seems luck is
on your side
they said
perhaps i replied
or maybe it is
because i am
on my side

sadness tends to be happy when
we allow ourselves to be sad
but happiness tends to be sad when
we don't allow ourselves to be happy

**self discovery
is self recovery**

ella zelensky

when i was 4 my observations
were too big for my vocabulary
eventually the level of my
mental age excelled beyond
my physical one
a bizarre experience
of feeling both disconnected and
deeply connected with my body
mind
heart
and soul
but when a 4 year old has the
equivalent of an inner universe
expanding at an inconceivable
rate within them
how can they describe what they
see when their peers can only
see within the observable universe

strange things are happening
things i struggle to explain
like dreaming of a plane
crashing into foreign terrain
guessing the exact reason
for someone else's pain
sensing the end of times when
innocent children are slain
or seeing a vision of the future
standing in the rain

it felt like being
hit by a car
a momentary flash of light
a loud vortex
a final phase
the click of a lock
vaporisation
strangeness
and everything
deeply unsettling

**perhaps they lived
because you noticed**

there's too much
to think about
to have nothing
to do

they called you a wallflower
but you were the only one
mature enough to bloom
what was the point of
owning the place when you
couldn't even read the room

-       underestimated for their awareness / feared for their awareness

i am made exactly how i was meant to be
if i was modelled over someone else
i wouldn't be unique

i'm not how you
wanted me to be
but that's okay
because i want
to be how i want to be

when we're different together
we are all the same

now i know that to get rid of
the past is to get rid of me
how can you get here
when you erase the path
that facilitated the outcome
how can you erase your existence

where will life take me
if i don't take me with it

if every second is an opportunity
to make the right decision
and a day still passes
without you making it
you have lost 86,400 chances
to change your life

ella zelensky

i fear the day
where each
increment
reaches what felt
like a distant end
because the years
are flying by like
pages in the wind
and i fear i have
been measuring
the wrong priorities

indescence

so many years were spent
walking in circles
that my concept of progress
was getting close enough
but consistently turning away

recently i realised that
there are a plethora of things
i would fear more than
going skydiving
it was a wakeup call
for what i prioritise in life

everything was fine
until the word
death was mentioned
suddenly the smile
faded from my face
my eyes widened
and i asked innocently
what do you mean
you see
love never ceases to
be love in the presence
of impermanence
perhaps impermanence
is a lighter way of
putting death
but what comes before
is what matters
and it is the tape of
sadness wound backwards
that plays love
the first
the final
and everything
in between

if i tie myself
to your memory
i think i get
to keep you
in reality it's grief
that keeps me
and i own nothing

ripping the clock
off the wall and
winding back
its arms until
your own start aching
changes nothing
you can't go to the past
no matter how many
times you or the clock
go around in circles

don't expect to grow inside
a space you have outgrown
why stay but stay unhappy
until you think
i should have known

the past is solidified but
the present is malleable

ella zelensky

don't wish for the past
that is why we say
it is past and gone

you're afraid of engaging
with the outside world
because you're afraid of
engaging with your
inner world
as long as you refuse
to become a better
communicator with both
you will continue to reject
and be rejected by both

you're not losing
you're experiencing
nothing is lost
when it is learnt

life may not be forever
but i like to think that
within the window we
are given
to live life until the end
is complete on its own
it is both a long and short
forever within the parameters
of human biology
so what more could you
ask for

remember that time
simply flows
and if you beg it
for answers
it is not its job
to know

there are no outcomes
if there are no decisions
make a choice

ella zelensky

i want to know love
what do i do
she asked
you love they said

weightlessness
my love
you are weightless
you hurt less
you get the first row
seat to the sky
way up high
only glory occupies
your big beautiful eyes
no more bruises
no more scars
just a gentle journey to
the moon and stars
i kiss you goodbye
and leave you to god
and if it's god who takes
you to heaven's door
i couldn't ask for more

ella zelensky

the path to heaven
is filled with children
skipping along a road
playing tic tac toe
laughing in groups
and planting flowers
in rows

you lied to us
he screamed
you lied to our
whole country
thousands of
kilometres away
in a foreign country
another man turned
around in shock
did you hear that
he asked those
around him
i heard an echo
saying you lied to us
i don't know the language
but i understood
exactly what he meant

ella zelensky

as the sun rises
the heat waves dance
and bodies strewn
across the streets
lay completely still from
their final goodnight

losing you will be
the end of me

it felt like a spaceship erupting in the
sky just to reach out and
hold your hand
it felt like the fight of my life to love you
you cried when you saw me cry
neon tears swimming in the air like raindrops
on car windows
sometimes when you hear absolutely nothing
but see everything it hurts more
i was afraid i would forget what you looked like
sounded like
felt like
but everything was burning up
dismantling
shaking violently
ready to fall apart
and suddenly it did
you were torn from me in the blink of an eye
thrown mercilessly in the opposite direction
i screamed at the stars for not doing anything
to save you
but i couldn't hear myself
so i resigned to death as you impacted the ocean
and our love immortalised forever

every cell in my body
wept deafeningly
when i missed
you by a centimetre
you are so close
yet out of reach
you are my pain
and my joy
the reason i breathe

ella zelensky

who knew a sign of love
would be seen
as an act of war

you can never forget
the sight of a face
whose eyes have
grown resentful
of the human race

ella zelensky

the leafless tree beckoned him
i see something in you it said
come to me
let me give you the rage your
heart pounds for
its branches swallow him like
a pit of snakes as a fire ignites in him
the glory of annihilation
exploding in his eyes
the drifting debris
the torturous screams
and the murdered
generations of people in his dreams
tempt him
he places the crown upon his head
and faces the world with arms raised
behold the devil of humankind
destroyer of earth
and ally of darkness

i'm sorry that i'm not looking
you in the eyes the child said
i'm trapped in a dark and scary cinema
that replays the death of all my people
and when the credits roll
i run to the screen and
frantically look for
the names of my family
but there are too many
names all at once
so i stay trapped in
this cinema for the sake
of looking for them in the dark
with all the other children
who are like me too
maybe one day they'll play this movie
at a big famous film festival
and they'll call out our names
for the awards we have won
but no one will come to collect them
the audience will grow
silent and ashamed as we die in our seats
and when the cinema doors
are finally opened
they will collect our bodies
our arms reached out to
the names we finally spotted in the credits

ella zelensky

it's okay if you
don't find my body
the dead child says
the angels found
my soul

you looked human
but that smile
is worn by the devil

ella zelensky

the chandelier
you love will
hold the diamonds
that fall and cut
you to pieces
royalty suits
your ego until
it all comes
crashing down

i dreamt about a lady
standing in the streets
handing out flyers
that said one world
one humanity
one world? she gestured
to every couple of people
one world?
one humanity?
the interactions were cold
no thank you
people said
sorry
i'm alright
no thanks
her eyes grew darker
with each rejection
and her hands trembled
from the weight of
the untaken flyers
was one world a fruitless aspiration?
was one humanity destined to fail?
the lady looked at her
flyers and wondered why
unity had to be advertised
on sheets of paper
in her determination she
called out
one world?
one humanity?
louder than before
but all i saw were people
ignoring her before waking up

it looked like the world
was ending
but wanted to be
beautiful one last time

we are a case study
for the aliens out there
we are the failed experiment
the negative outcome
the philosophy that
backfired on itself
we are the world that
takes life for granted
and now we pay the price
for playing dice

ella zelensky

we have been violent
since the beginning
we crave our own
destruction

may you awaken
in the hidden land
of tall trees and
soft grass
may the butterflies
follow your every
step as you
leap and bound
through the forest
may the doe your
name signifies
remain in your spirit
as this new place
loves you more than
the other one could
you will not be sprayed
by hundreds of bullets like
you were on earth
you won't wait in a car
for hours with the
phone to your ear
there is only healing
and only peace here
you are free
you are with destiny now

-in memory of hind rajab

do you not see it glistening in their eyes?
the keys to their house?
the keys to their land?
the keys to their history?
you bind their hands and muzzle their mouths
cut up their bodies and cackle as you set them ablaze
but before you can rejoice in your false win
you see their soul stand upright from
within the flames and look directly at you
do you not see it glistening in their eyes?
the keys to their house?
the keys to their land?
the keys to their history?
you stagger back and scream
as they walk out of the flames
the keys dangling in their hand
just a second ago you thought
they were clenched in your fist
but the truth doesn't like to play games like that
you thought you could incinerate the evidence
but while a body can be burned a memory cannot
and fire only fuels memory

do you hear it in the air
the revolution against the fascists
the pound of the drum
as her eyes look up
with conviction
buckets of paint thrown
at the walls
reclaiming their voices
they say the anonymous
spray painters are the
secret messengers of our time
the enemy stands tall
at the podium looking down
but staggers back in horror
as the sea of spectators
raise their eyes in unison
we are the revolution

ella zelensky

there is no other side
to stand beside
when it's genocide

when i asked a question
you questioned my question
upon further investigation
i found out you are a robot
with designated responses

if the information
makes them angrier
then it will make
them happier

-self-serving argument

remain the person
who humbles others

people will give you
what you want at the
price of your awareness

we speak of betrayal being unfair
despite being its originator

ella zelensky

i fear a future where we depart
earth and watch
as she frowns deeply because
we are no longer in need of her
we are cruel
we are exploitative
we are human

justice will be the day
where everything sits
in front of us in the
courtroom of the afterlife

that is how the world works
people muzzle the person
they don't want to speak
or to really seal the act
they simply kill them off

-the abuser that got away

usually death is involuntary
but with the
current state of the world
the ratio is evening

for the first time
in my life
i stayed up all night
and into the morning
without a blink of sleep
we don't think about
the earth turning
when we're busy
living out the day
but there was something
profound about
witnessing the earth
spin back to face
the sun again

the ticking of time outlives
the beating of any human heart
but one thing that does run
parallel to the passage of time
is the love those hearts pass on
that is why time and love
are old friends

ella zelensky

in my motherhood
i imagine the words
look what i did
by my children
will be one of my
proudest moments

i can run because
you believed in my
first steps as a child

belief is where running
turns into flight

god made the sun so
we could see each other
god made the sun so that
everything and everyone
could live on earth
god made the sun
and because of it you are
burnt into my memory

ella zelensky

with a weakening spirit
and tired eyes
the sun pulses softly
as it gradually dies
i did the best i could
it says
i lived for you to live
forgive me it cries
and i say
there is nothing to forgive
you were the light
of our lives
and by nature our lives
must eventually die

it's good that you can cry
it means you have memories

ella zelensky

forever will never omit
the fear of goodbye

the passing down
of facial features
is beautiful
it means when
you look in the mirror
you see who you loved

ella zelensky

it is no coincidence that
my pen ran out of ink
as i was writing about
everything i love about you

there is beauty in not
being able to find a
word to describe you
it means you outrun
the dictionary

ella zelensky

definitions are beautiful tools
they describe things that
captivate us so that we can
draw upon them to be
reminded of that feeling again
but definitions are
also limiting
they confine things to
a designated description
and offer a few synonyms
until it's time for the next
word in the list
so whilst i love definitions
as a poet whose expectation
is to utilise them
i often find myself needing
to step away from definitions
so i can take in the world
without the parameters of input

indescence

when you cross
a quiet person
with unexpected
intellect
they make sure
they become the
loudest voice
in your head

ella zelensky

to have and to hold
they say
but even though you
wanted to have me
you never wanted
to hold me

they asked if
i loved you

i will leave my answer
to the question

i had to learn that you were
not my shoulder to cry on
but rather the one who had been
giving me the cold shoulder all along

iridescence

i handed you a string
and you returned
with scissors
i thought you were
cutting the rope to
make the distance
between us smaller
to make our love
even closer
but scissors don't
work like that
and every gesture i made
was an opportunity
for you to continue
cutting until we were
too difficult to hold onto

you never wanted
our picture in a frame
whilst i saw it as commitment
you saw it as a box
now when i see pictures of you
i am glad i am not part of them

they wanted you to stay
for the show just to
get you to pay for it
it's all a performance
and they got exactly
what they wanted from you

charming or disarming
it's your call to make

we shouldn't have
to pick petals
from flowers
to determine whether
someone loves us
the flowers did
nothing wrong
they took precious
time to grow
and we murder them
for no reason
whether he loves you
or loves you not
should never end
in destroying anything
or anyone around you
if he makes you
that unsure that
suffering ensues
he probably isn't
the one

you tried advertising your love
but you don't pay for a soulmate

perhaps you would have met
a different version of me
if you had met me in
a different season
a different place
or a different time
perhaps if i was in
a better stage in my life
i would be yours and
you would be mine

ella zelensky

three words
two people
one chance
and zero taken
unfortunately
many people
end up this way
even though they
are deeply in love
with no one else

if i have to die waiting
for the right man
instead of being with
someone i love
half-heartedly
i swear i will wait

ella zelensky

you played chess
with the
wrong person
because i
knew how
to play it too
you relied on
all the tactics
i knew the counter
movements to
so i knocked
over each of your
pieces and you
realised you
had fallen
but i had fallen too
i fell in love
with you

i can't stand you precisely
because you make me a
better person
it's not that i can't avoid you
it's that with you
i cannot avoid myself
and that is why i follow you
because i like who i become
in your presence

you could have never calculated that
we would fall in love like this
you look at me with furrowed eyebrows
taken aback because you cannot read me
as quickly as you read your study papers
i frustrate you
i enamour you
i occupy you
you try to divert your attention but
my symphony always finds its way to you
you've never lost track of your thoughts like this before
you hate to admit your distraction
so you contemplate your subtraction from the attraction
but you are astounded by a second defeat
that is how you and i meet

when a creative soul collides with
another creative soul
a seismic event occurs
the sky dips into different colours
and the universe rumbles
two painters
two harmonies
two artists who fell in love
hanging colours in the air like lanterns
and the world shimmers like
humanity has never witnessed before
art is a kind of love
and love is a kind of art

ella zelensky

you
my love
are like synesthesia

iridescence

i used to be so numb
i became indifferent
unloved and tossed around
in circles for being different
flowers didn't sing to me
and the sun was not my friend
i thought it was cruel how
life didn't seem to end
that in the dying of a flower
its neck began to bend
but before i could no
longer tread in the deep end
you appeared
a godsend
you were warm
at first my frosted skin
burned at your touch
i shrilled violently inside because
the opposite feeling meant
feeling too much
but it took your love to learn
that you weren't burning me alive
you were thawing me so i
could stay alive
so the numbness finally
transitioned to feeling
and the feeling finally
transitioned to healing
and when i could finally look
you in the eyes
you reminded me what a
kiss felt like

like fumbling your way
out of the darkness
when you call out your
soulmate's name enough times
you will eventually
find one another

you raised my standards
and taught me that there
are others out there
who will meet them
you taught me rarity
but not scarcity

ella zelensky

i can wait a minute
a minute doesn't seem like much
but a minute won't wait for us
suddenly someone has lived
forty four million six hundred
and twenty six thousand minutes
and suddenly you only have one minute
to say goodbye
or maybe only 44 seconds
but the doctors did not lie
nor did time
it is human beings that act like
forty four million minutes could
succeed the test of time
but when you only have 44 seconds left
to love them on earth
there are no backup minutes
to delay the way you will hurt

if you had to
travel space
alone with
one person
who would
you choose as
your companion

i have never wanted anything
more than this
i have waited eras for you
i have lived every time period
every catastrophe
every day
and every night
to walk outside my door and see
my destiny across the street
bow in hair and flowers in hand
the sunlight illuminating
every floating strand
begging god for you to turn around
and eventually you did
your eyes pulled me in like a string
and when my body soared towards you
when you pulled me in
the world erupted into artistry
together we spun and began
our destiny

*what's taking you
so long* his
mother asked
*ask her
your eyes tell
me all i need
to know*

it's possible to
to make her yours
if you don't resign
to letting her go
so run the extra mile
and knock on her door
drive across the country
and if you have to
even more
hand your ticket over and
catch the plane
your heart won't
stop until you hear her
call your name
so make her yours
make her yours
make her yours

indescence

the question you need
to ask yourself is
what will you lose in
your lifetime if you
choose not to tell them
how will the regret
of not saying it steal
the light from your soul
and plant misery
in your bones

if i'm trying to
hide it all
then i'm trying
to hide myself

what are we to do with the
intensity of this love
you suffocate
me when you're
in the same room and yet
you fill my lungs with air
when you're
here i can't be near you
yet when you're not here i need
you there

and so began the tension of
their unspoken romance
when she took his hand
in the ice-skating rink
the confession began
it all circles back to you
they said as they circled
around one another
carving out elaborate
orbits and maps that created
the guide to their feelings
wearing shoes that
could make you fly
so god could send you
to map the skies with them
they spun hand in hand
faster and faster
until they felt the feeling
of being in union

the power of dreams is that
they tell you the truth
when you're too afraid to
think about it voluntarily

you are always running away
because you want to be loved
but that's not how you are loved

if you have no feelings
there's nothing to steal
but will you remove them
at the cost of the ability to feel

no one iris is the same in
this world yet i see
all of humanity in yours
no pattern of one's
fingertips in this world
resembles anyone else's
only yours trace
the roadmap to your love

i understand the
word soulmate
but with you
i feel it

ella zelensky

i listened
to the melody
once more
and was no
longer afraid
of life moving
forward

in the grand scheme
of the universe
the earth is but one star
we are
a miracle inside a miracle
as time went on we
figured out what love meant
called it a name and felt it deeply
we make earth what earth is
so in the grand scheme
of the universe
the earth may look
like just another planet
enveloped in darkness
but the special thing
about earth is that it's
filled with people who
exist for love
science is one way
of seeing the universe
but love
love is the final touch

if everyone was the same
the world would stay the same
but when everyone is different
we are able to make a difference

i could attempt poetry of grandeur
but do my words have to be
the best moments that humbled me
happened unexpectedly
to love and be loved
in this magnificent odyssey
is the purest definition of
what it means to be free
put simply
the space between you and me
and the time we share indefinitely
is what humanity must
hold onto tightly
you fear death like you fear the
vastness of the darkness because you
fear whether we die peacefully
but faith endures exponentially
and i have found it is enough

ella zelensky

indescence

About the Author

Ella is an Australian published author and current university student at the University of Queensland. In her BA she majored in anthropology, and also studied religion, sociology and intercultural communication. She is currently in her final semester of a Masters in International Relations.

Since she was young, culture, race, religion, language, cinematography, and activism have played a significant role in her creative work and academic studies. After struggling with fitting in during her early high school years, writing poetry helped her cope and rise above. Writing eventually became serious to her and she began sharing her work on her social media platform. Ella published her first poetry book,
Little Dreamer in March of 2021.

Her dream to be a humanitarian worker, as well as interests in education, mental health and equality inspire many of her poems and quotes. Through Ella's passion for people, reform, and harmony, she wishes to help others own their identity, take a stand, forgive, unite, and ultimately heal.

In 2018 Ella launched The Leadlight Project, as a creative hub for teens struggling with social isolation and loneliness. The Projects aim, to gather identified teens to develop and create artwork, poetry, short films, and photography to be showcased and celebrated at a collaborative exhibition, scheduled for the 12th of October 2019, in conjunction with QLD Mental Health.

Unfortunately, due to ongoing illness, Ella had to place the Project's collaborative Exhibitions on hold. In 2021, the re-formatted project relaunched via a new Shopfront whereby a percentage of sales will be donated to children's charities dear to Ella's heart, including Unicef's Yemen Crisis.

www.ellazelensky.com

© Ella Zelensky, 2025. All rights reserved

www.ingramcontent.com/pod-product-compliance
Lightning Source LLC
Chambersburg PA
CBHW012208090526
44583CB00023BA/2966